PAPER PEONY PRESS

Beauty Truth & Goodness

DEVOTIONAL FOR TEEN GIRLS

Thanks so much for buying our book!
For a free extra, email

paperpeonypress@gmail.com

and we will send something
fun to your inbox!

We would love to see how you're using your this devotional...
snap a picture and tag us!
@paperpeonypress

BEAUTY, TRUTH & GOODNESS
© Paper Peony Press.
First Edition, 2022

Published by: Paper Peony Press
www.paperpeonypress.com

For wholesale inquiries contact: reagan@paperpeonypress.com

Printed in China

ISBN - 978-1-952842-88-7

To Ma, a woman of God, a messenger of God, and a Daughter of God. Thank you for being my cheerleader.

Love, Olivia

INTRODUCTION

Before I was invited to write this devotional, I had a dream. In my dream there was a large group of ladies of all ages, from young girls to older women walking together toward a destination that I was not looking at because I already knew that they were marching toward Jesus. Some of the faces were familiar to me, while other faces I had never seen before, but they all were glowing and strong, focused and determined. Then I heard God speak to me and say, "These are my daughters, they are citizens of Heaven and they will know their language, they will know the True Word of God. They will not be swayed by this world, they will not be deterred by lies, distractions, or obstacles because they will be rooted in the truth of the Bible." I thought that it just meant that I was to help God by encouraging my sisters at church and in my community - with kind, uplifting words - to read the Bible. But here we are, a devotional with stories that God has given me to share, each one pointing back to the True Word of the Mighty God of All!

What I hope you find in these passages are sparks that ignite your curiosity to open your Bible by yourself, with a friend, or with a group of friends and read deeper into God's True word, and get to know your language. I hope that you experience a thirst for a better understanding of who God is and who He says you are. When you read the living Word of God, you are drawing nearer to Him, and when you draw near to Him, God will reveal Himself and His plans to you. He is waiting for you to spend time with Him; He has made you "for such a time as this" (Esther 4:14) to join in building His kingdom on Earth as it is in Heaven. Only you can do what He has gifted you to do; you will find out what your gifts are when you spend time in the Word and you talk with God. My deepest hope and highest prayer is that you, dear sister, see our Father for the truly wonderful Dad that He is and that you are able to receive His invitation to partner with Him and be about setting other people free.

-Des Leiloglou

CONTENTS

CALLED TO BE A PEACEMAKER

MICAH 6:8

Mankind, he has told each of you what is good and what it is the LORD requires of you: to act justly, to love faithfulness, and to walk humbly with your God.

Micah 6:8

I have a friend named Kelly. She is a little older than me, and when we get to talk, she often asks questions to know how I am doing. One time when we were on the phone, Kelly shared a powerful observation that God was revealing to her over and over again throughout her week. She said, "You know what, Des? We—all of God's children—are looking to be offended. We are just waiting for someone to offend us in our day! And that's not what God has created us to be like." Kelly went on to share a short story with me from her week. As she walked through a hall at her work, she said hello to her friends and co-workers as she passed, but one of those friends didn't reply or smile back at her. The friend didn't seem to be the same, like something was wrong. Kelly proceeded through her day but she couldn't stop thinking about her friend and wondering, "Did I do something to hurt her? Did I say hello aggressively? Was she hurt by something else that I may have done?"

As Kelly was thinking about this friend, she started to get angry and mentally defend herself.

"Well, she might have thought that I should have come to her first to tell her 'Hi!'"

"She might be mad because I didn't invite her to lunch yesterday?"

Then Kelly noticed herself getting mad at her friend when she didn't even know for sure if anything was wrong with this friend, much less if Kelly had offended her. Kelly realized how sneaky and stealthy the enemy was in trying to steal her joy, kill her unity with her friend, and destroy their friendship. So she walked into her friend's office and asked her how she was and then told her what had happened. Kelly's friend admitted that she was, in fact, struggling with some things but it had nothing to do with Kelly or work. Kelly's friend proceeded to apologize to her for causing confusion and then asked her for prayer for her personal situation.

Kelly shared with me what God had been showing her, that as daughters of the one true God, we are called to be peacemakers! We are called to do the often time-consuming tasks of talking to people who look angry, confused, frustrated, or sad, and taking care of them, especially our brothers and sisters in Christ. When we ourselves have hurt or angered one of our sisters or brothers, we are supposed to go to them and talk it out, apologize, and amend our mistake.

GOD,

Help me to be a peacemaker with the people in my life. Help me to boldly seek reconciliation with others, and if I am not the one who has offended, use me to promote peace. Let your love flow through me to others and grow me to not be easily offended by others.

AMEN.

FOLLOWING THE LEADER

PHILIPPIANS 2:14–15

Do everything without grumbling or arguing, so that you may become blameless and pure, "children of God without fault in a warped and crooked generation." Then you will shine among them like stars in the sky.

Philippians 2:14–15

In Numbers 16, we learn that Korah, along with his friends Dathan and Abiram, rebel against God by challenging Moses and Aaron, whom God had called to be the leaders. We don't know why God chose Moses and Aaron, but he did, and used them to save his people from Pharaoh and deliver them from slavery in Egypt. God has

his reasons and we know that he knows best and is always right and good.

In this situation, Korah was mad that Moses and Aaron were in charge.

Have you ever questioned a parent or teacher, coach, or organization leader, even just in your head? Have you ever wondered, "Why would you pick her to lead? Why is she the captain? What does she have that makes her better than me?"
Have you ever leaned over to another teammate and shared these thoughts? Ever started conversations with other group members about how your leader or captain was lacking or (in your opinion) not quite good enough?

If so, it might be worth considering how you may have allowed pride in your heart to mutate your thoughts toward complaining and grumbling. If you find that your heart is in that state, then it may also be worth considering how that may be preventing you from being used by God.

This type of sin in your life can act like a contagious virus that will infect others on your team or organization. In effect, you are saying that your coach, teacher, parent, or leader doesn't know as much as you do! Is that true? Do you know more than an adult doing whatever activity you're involved in does? I have felt this way before, questioned why a particular girl was chosen to be the captain of my softball team. I have felt angry because I thought I was a better choice to lead the photography department of the yearbook. But in reflecting on these incidents, I realize that I was only focusing on me and what was not given to me. I was not focused on the needs of my team or organization and what was best for the whole. I was not considering the chosen leader, and how they might be the better choice.

Korah basically told God that he made a mistake in picking Moses and Aaron to lead the Israelites. Korah really thought that he knew more than God! Because of his arrogant heart and grumbling attitude, God opened the earth and swallowed him and his co-conspirators (Dathan and Abiram), as well as all of their families.

Humbling ourselves is hard, and following others is hard. But if we keep our eyes on Jesus and off of our fears, doubts, and worldly distractions, God will help us obey. Instead of critiquing and criticizing others on your team or in your organization, you could create! Create suggestions on how to better your team, fix a problem, or strengthen a weakness. Be an encourager, a cheerleader for your teammates and your coaches and leadership. Join with them instead of grumbling and complaining against them. Just like Paul encouraged the early churches in Galatia, "And let us not grow weary of doing good, for in due season we will reap, if we do not give up" (Galatians 6:9, ESV).

LORD GOD,

Forgive me if I have been jealous and have spoken badly about someone else when I have disagreed. Forgive me for wanting to lift myself into an important role before a leader has appointed me to that position. Help me to be a helper and an asset to my team or organization, Father, and grow me in maturity to repent and to ask for forgiveness if I fall into temptation.

AMEN.

We are weak, but He is strong!

2 CORINTHIANS 12:10

So, I take pleasure in weaknesses, insults, hardships, persecutions, and in difficulties, for the sake of Christ. For when I am weak, then I am strong.

2 Corinthians 12:10

God never promised that he wouldn't give us more than we can handle in our lifetimes. There's more proof of this fact throughout the Bible and in particular, in the apostle Paul's life. Paul experienced "pressures and troubles" that he described as "far beyond our ability to endure, so that we despaired of life itself" (2 Corinthians 1:8b).

When we accept the free gift of salvation through Jesus's sacrifice, we should expect that as we go through life, we will experience pressures and troubles. The difference in living a Christ-filled life is that we have the one true God who is our leader and helper. We can ask God to take away these troubles when they arise, but sometimes those troubles are meant for a greater purpose. In the book of 2 Corinthians, Paul describes these pressures and troubles as "thorns in my side" and he prays to God often to take them away. God answers Paul, "My grace is sufficient for you, for my power is perfected in weakness" (2 Corinthians 12:9 CSB). God essentially tells Paul, "No, I won't remove these troubles, because in them, I will make amazing things happen in the middle of your weakness and the glory will be given back to me."

This is why Paul delights in his weakness, in the insults and doubts, in the hardships and persecution from others, and in the difficulties that he experienced. Because all the glory and honor will go to God because of and in spite of Paul's human weakness. It has always been, and will always be, about bringing glory to God, pointing back to God, and allowing God to guide his children back to him by whichever means God chooses. And sometimes God chooses little ol' us.

Do you have pressures, challenges, or difficulties in your life today? A difficult leader? A mean person who says harsh words to you? A challenging class, subject, task, or project? Something that is stopping you from fully engaging in the work that God has called you to do?

You might feel like these difficulties are beyond you, and that is exactly the point: Hand them over to God and let him show you what only he can do! It will impact more than just you; it will impact his kingdom.

FATHER,

May my weakness lead to a greater reliance on you. Forgive me for stepping in your rightful place in my life as leader. Help me to submit to your way and follow you in whichever direction you guide me. Help others to see your glory as you work through my weakness. You are so good.

AMEN.

CITIZEN OF HEAVEN

EPHESIANS 2:19

So then you are no longer strangers and aliens, but you are fellow citizens with the saints and members of the household of God.

Ephesians 2:19

If you call Jesus Christ your Savior—if you believe that he sacrificed his perfect self to cleanse you of your sin and unrighteousness—then you are a child of God. Because you belong to God, you are a citizen of Heaven! This is the citizenship that really matters because it is eternal; it will last forever. After your physical body passes away, it won't matter if you're a United States citizen, a Mexican citizen, French citizen, or citizen of Mars. Those citizenships will be done. Even now, earthly citizenships can be denied, rejected, and revoked. But once you have received Jesus's gift of eternal life, you are a citizen of Heaven. The language of this beautiful place is the Word of God, the Bible! You can learn, grow, and get to know God each and every day just by sitting down and reading the Bible. You do not need fancy Bible studies, or special circumstances to sit down and read the Word. All you need is a little light, your Bible, and just a little bit of time. You might say, "I don't understand some of the stories that I have read. The names are hard to pronounce and I am not sure what the story I read was about." If that's you, let me let you in on a little secret for y'all: Some of us adults are dealing with the exact same problems. Generous elders have advised me to first ask God for help in prayer, and let him direct me to wisdom. I could also ask God to provide me with someone who knows more than I do about the Bible, a discipler who I can text questions to or call and discuss whatever it is I have read. I could even look for commentaries written by believers who have studied the Bible in seminary. God provides resources and all we have to do is ask him for help to see them and access them! The Bible Project is another trusted and wonderful visual resource. If you do better listening to the Bible, you can listen to the Bible being read to you on The Bible App on any smartphone. There are so many ways that you can access and be immersed in God's Word. In different seasons of your life, one method may be what you need over another, and God is good to always provide what we need when we are in need of it!

FATHER,

Thank you for your pursuit of me and for providing all that I need and more to learn from you. Your encouragement and open invitation to join you each and every day by reading the Bible is more than generous. Thank you for teaching me the truth and loving me so well.

AMEN.

LIVING WATER

JOHN 7:37–38

On the last day of the feast, the great day, Jesus stood up and cried out, "If anyone thirsts, let him come to me and drink. Whoever believes in me, as the Scripture has said, 'Out of his heart will flow rivers of living water.'"

John 7:37–38

In the Middle East, the majority of people practice Islam. They know about Jesus and they believe that he was a prophet, but their holy leader was a man named Mohammed. I want to tell you a story I heard, about a nomadic herder who lives in the Middle Eastern desert. The man had no electricity, plumbing, satellite, or internet. His job was herding animals, such as camels and sheep; he lived a solitary life. One day a missionary came to this man, and the man told the missionary an amazing story: "Each night a man wearing all white comes to my home and tells me to write these things down." The missionary opened this man's notebook and read, "In the beginning was the Word, and the Word was with God, and the Word was God" (John 1:1). Jesus had been coming every night to this man in the desert and had been giving him the book of John.

Yes, that book of John, the last of the four gospels in the New Testament. How amazing is God? He pursues all of his precious people to the ends of earth by any and all means necessary. And that means that he will and is doing this for you, dear reader! He will never stop chasing after you. His desire is to be with you in every moment of every day. If you haven't received his gift and want to, all you have to do is say a simple prayer like this:

God, I don't understand everything, but I believe that you sent your perfect Son Jesus to die as a sacrifice for my sins, and that he was raised from the dead and he has invited me into your family. I accept this as truth and as my gift. I am your child, God. Thank you, Lord! Amen.

Now, like John 7:38 said, you, sweet sister (because we are sisters now, in this big family of God's), will flow rivers of living water from your heart.

GOD,

Allow me to boldly go out into your world and proclaim your love and the good news, not just with words but also with my actions and the way that I love others. Flow through me, Lord, that living water, and help me to refresh others who are in need. Give me courage to go to the places you need me to be and allow me to be a blessing.

AMEN.

DO NOT LET ANYONE

LOOK DOWN ON YOU

BECAUSE YOU ARE

YOUNG

BUT SET AN

EXAMPLE

FOR THE BELIEVERS

AND IN PURITY.

1 TIM. 4:12

IN SPEECH, IN CONDUCT,

IN LOVE, IN FAITH

Weekly Reflection

GOD IS OUR HERO

PROVERBS 3:5

Trust in the LORD with all your heart and lean not on your own understanding; in all your ways submit to him, and he will make your paths straight.

Proverbs 3:5-6

Have you ever heard or read the story of Esther? I used to think that it was a women's empowerment story that taught me to fight for a seat at the table and prove that girls can help, too. However, I recently dug into the book of Esther and God graciously showed

me some things I had not seen before. First of all, Esther and her older cousin/adoptive father, Mordecai, were courageous, God-loving people, but they are not the heroes of the story. Yes, they did brave things and they were obedient, but the only true hero in this story is God himself. He's not mentioned once throughout the book of Esther, but he is very much present.

The story of Esther opens with a corrupt and powerful king, Xerxes, who is reigning over a huge swath of land and people, and his advisors are equally horrid. One particular advisor named Haman is set on killing the whole Jewish population in King Xerxes' kingdom. Meanwhile, Esther becomes queen, wife to King Xerxes, and Mordecai tells her that she must speak up for her people, the Jewish people in her kingdom. Time after time, God makes it so that everything Queen Esther asks for is given to her. She is shown extreme favor, even though she is put into some scary and worrisome situations. By her actions, Esther shows that she believes in who God says he is, because at one crucial point she asks all of the Jewish people to fast and pray. To fast is to go to spiritual war and to declare trust in God's full control, power, and leadership; that's what Esther did and what she asked her people to do, too. She leaned on the Lord and trusted that only God would and could save her and her people from total destruction and annihilation, and he did! Esther's and Mordecai's faithfulness are an example for us today, reminding us that we can trust God's protection and deliverance.

GOD,

You said that you will make a way for us and make our paths straight. Help us believe that and preach it to ourselves. Give us courage, Lord, to boldly obey your promptings and allow us to be brilliant lights that shine your love on the world around us, giving all the credit to you and your Son, Jesus.

AMEN.

ALL THE GLORY TO GOD

1 THESSALONIANS 4:11–12

Aspire to lead a calm and peaceful life as you mind your own business and earn your living, just as we've taught you. By doing this you will live an honorable life, influencing others and commanding respect of even the unbelievers.

1 Thessalonians 4:11–12

I struggle with not being recognized and not being given credit. If I do something cool, like say something powerful, or share a deep thought, but don't get credit for it, I can boil with frustration and resentment. For example, I shared a favorite song with a friend, and then the next week that friend showed up with tickets to see that band. They told everyone who would listen about the song that I had shared with them, as if they had discovered the band themselves. They didn't even say, "Des showed me this band. This was her favorite song and I love it too." Another time, I shared with some friends a lesson God had been working on in me and instead of acknowledging that I shared something with them, they claimed the lesson as their own.

Why can't my friends and peers give me acknowledgement for my awesomeness? I really do feel this way sometimes, and I would leave Bible studies and hangouts feeling deflated.

I talked to my best friend, who lovingly comforted and reassured me, but one day, I realized I hadn't ever brought my frustration to God. I think I felt ashamed that I wanted the credit, like maybe wanting credit was wrong and how could I ask God for something that was wrong? This was my problem that I needed to get over; I needed to not be bothered by wanting the credit. I then remembered that God wants me to tell Him all of it, even my prayers that may be wrong.

I finally asked God to help my heart. Whatever wound I had that wanted to be seen and given credit, I wanted Him to heal it. Change my desire, help me to not be frustrated, help me to not want to get the credit. And while I was crying, I heard Him out of the complete silence say, "*Give it away. Give it away. Give it away.*"

God, in the most loving and gentle way, was showing me that all those things I did and said, all the shares and deep thoughts, were good, but only because they came from him. Those good things were His that He gave to me to share. I was to give every single one of those good things to my sisters and brothers and then give any credit (whenever I would get credit) back to God! God was telling me to not worry about the credit, not worry about being seen or recognized or praised.

GOD,

We were made by you and for you. Help us to be brilliant beams of light so that we can bring glory and attention to you. Thank you for always wanting to hear our pains, desires, and troubles, even if we are in the wrong. Father, you want all of our prayers so you can help us be more like your Son. Thank you for your loving mercy and generous grace.

AMEN.

NEW CREATION

2 CORINTHIANS 5:17

Therefore, if anyone is in Christ, the new creation has come: The old has gone, the new is here!

2 Corinthians 5:17

Do you have any friends that are really good at something? My friend Lauren is really good at dancing. When she hears music, she starts to move and she makes everyone around her look good dancing, too! Lauren also fiercely loves the Lord and it is evident by how she loves her family and friends. Lauren is a part of a community of women that I am a part of and we have been able to spend time together weekly. During one of our meetings, Lauren, who is normally quiet and reserved, spoke with loving and encouraging authority when a discussion arose about us being children of God and sinners. The person sharing her thoughts was focusing on the fact that we are all wretched sinners who are not worthy. Lauren reminded all of us that yes, we are all in fact sinners who have fallen short of the glory of God, but we have been redeemed, chosen, and covered by Jesus—we have been made new! As new creations, we do not need to continue to beat ourselves up about who we used to be; rather, we have got things to do for the Lord. Lauren is right; it is important to always remember that we were once lost and God found us and offered us his Son. If we accept his free gift of eternal life, then we are no longer identifiable as unclean or unworthy; we now share in the identity and blessing that God gave us in Jesus. We have jobs to do, sisters! We were each made for this specific point in time, with our specific gifts to do our specific jobs that God has directed us to. Let's be about our Father's work.

LORD,

I thank you for loving me so much that you sent your perfect Son as a sacrifice to pay my debt. Thank you for your great mercy and endless reminders that I am yours and you see me as worthy because of Jesus. Help me to receive my identity and the truth that you say about me. Let me be a blessed reminder to my friends and family of their identity and power in Christ.

AMEN.

GOD'S WAYS ARE BETTER

LUKE 15:32

It was fitting to celebrate and be glad, for this your brother was dead, and is alive; he was lost, and is found.

Luke 15:32

What comes to mind when you think of the book of Jonah in the Old Testament? If you're anything like me, your mind might go straight to how Jonah disobeyed God and was swallowed by a big fish! But Jonah's story has plenty to tell us about comparison, bitterness, and wanting God to act according to our own sense of justice.

Jonah was an Israelite, one of God's chosen people. Jonah had lost some family and friends to warring neighbors who wanted to enslave them. One neighbor group that was doing this was the Ninevites, who were a particularly brutal and wicked part of the Assyrian empire. They didn't worship God; they worshiped false gods that demanded horrible sacrifices, like their own children. Knowing their aggression first hand, Jonah did not want to go to Nineveh. On top of that, he knew they had killed some of his own family members and friends. Now God was asking Jonah to go to Nineveh and deliver to them a message of repentance from him.

But you know the story. Jonah disobeyed, and tried to run away to Tarshish. After Jonah rebelled and then apologized to God, he was spit out of the big fish, then he was off to Nineveh to complete the task God had given him. All he had to do was to proclaim in the city: "In forty days Nineveh will be demolished!" As soon as Jonah spoke this sentence, the people of Nineveh believed in God. The whole city, from the lowest slave all the way up to the king of Nineveh, repented of their wrongdoing, violence, and false worship of other gods—all of it. They wore sackcloth, fasted, and prayed earnestly to God. God forgave the whole city and 120,000 people were saved.

But rather than rejoicing at their salvation, Jonah was angry that God had shown the Ninevites favor. He could not see the goodness of God because his focus was on his own fear, bitterness, anger, and unforgiveness. But God met him there. God made a plant grow over where Jonah was sitting to give him shade, then God made a worm destroy the plant. Jonah was angry that the plant was killed, but God was showing Jonah that this group of people was more valuable than this plant, and that Jonah's bitterness would not let him see their true value.

The compassion, mercy, and generosity that God shows Jonah is beautiful. God is a patient and loving Father to Jonah and to us, and he always cares about our hearts understanding and obeying. Even when others hurt us, we are to forgive and trust that God will handle the justice; we are to continue in the tasks that he has for us and not get distracted by the attempts of the evil one to steal our focus. No matter the degree to which others have hurt us, God has us.

LORD,

Let us rejoice when those who once were lost are found, those who once were mean are forgiven and humbled, those who once were hurt are healed and transformed to healers. We proclaim that you, Father, are in the business of redemption and so are we. Forgive us when we don't want to forgive others and when we don't want to obey you. Strengthen us to listen to you calling us and to follow your directions. Use us mightily, God.

AMEN.

GOING AGAINST THE CROWD

JOHN 14:23

Jesus answered, "If anyone loves me, he will keep my word. My Father will love him, and we will come to him and make our home with him."

John 14:23

The book of Daniel is another book in the Old Testament, and takes place when Israel was held captive by the Babylonians. When the Babylonians captured people, they picked out all of the smart, promising people and forced them to work with the Babylonian king to make the empire better and stronger. The first chapter of Daniel records how they did this with Daniel and his three friends: Hananiah, Misheal, and Azariah. However, you may know these three friends better by their Babylonian names: Shadrach, Meshach, and Abednego. While King Nebuchadnezzar and his chief eunuch Ashpenaz trained these friends, along with others they captured, they would feed them and house them and get them ready to serve the king. The food that the Babylonians offered the men did not follow Jewish food laws, so the four friends asked

Ashpenaz if they could be tested for ten days on a different diet of vegetables and water.

Because God had granted Daniel favor, Ashpenaz agreed. At the end of the ten days, all four of the men looked healthier than the other captives who were eating the king's food. The men were allowed to continue with their diet and honor God's law. Everything that Daniel, Hananiah, Misheal, and Azariah did was always first filtered through honoring God. Can you imagine? Instead of choosing the easy path of assimilating and going along with what everyone else was doing, these four young men chose God, despite their seemingly hopeless situation.

What a wonderful example for us today. We are free to revere God so much that our response is like theirs: "but even if God does not, we will still serve him fully" (Daniel 3:18, paraphrased). Even in my unfavorable situation, in my need or want, in the discomfort and inconvenience, I will faithfully serve my God.

We live in a time with many cultural norms that are opposite of what God says honors him. Sometimes we make excuses and join the crowd to call those cultural norms OK. We need to remember the "God Filter": what honors God over everything else.

GOD OF THE UNIVERSE,

You were able to work through these devoted men and show us generations later what it looks like to love God in joyful obedience. Lord, make me bold in following you when everyone else seems to be doing something different. Let me know you more to see you clearer so that I can know your voice and stand firm in the things you've asked me to do. I love you, Lord.

AMEN.

BE STRONG AND

TAKE HEART

PSALM 31:24

Weekly Reflection

PUTTING OTHERS FIRST

ROMANS 15:4

For whatever was written in former days was written for our instruction, that through endurance and through the encouragement of the Scriptures we might have hope.

Romans 15:4

Jesus was tempted by Satan, the father of lies. Right after Jesus was baptized in the Jordan River by his cousin, John the Baptist, God sent a dove to fly over Jesus, and God tells Jesus and all who were around, "This is my beloved Son, with whom I am well pleased" (Matthew 3:17, ESV). Jesus is then led by the Spirit to the desert for forty days and nights to be tempted by the devil. You can read more about this in Matthew 4:1-11, but the gist of it is that the devil throws all he has at Jesus. He tempts Jesus by saying things like, "You're hungry, turn these stones into bread. You're true royalty and your Father is God, so throw yourself from the top of the temple and he will save you. You want power and stuff? Look at all these kingdoms; worship me and I will give them to you."

With each challenge the devil spoke, Jesus responded with an answer from the Bible:

"It is written: 'Man must not live on bread alone but on every word that comes from the mouth of God.'" (Deut. 8:3 CSB)

"It is also written: 'Do not test the LORD your God.'" (Deut 6:16 CSB)

"Go away Satan! For it is written: 'Worship the Lord your God, and serve only him.'" (Deut. 6:13 CSB)

Jesus showed us how to battle in our times of trial by going back to the Word of God. For example, one area where I am regularly tempted is to serve myself before serving others. I can develop a mindset that tells me that I am the most important person in the world. It's a downward spiral. But when I go back to the Bible, I can find correction for my bad habit: "Do nothing out of selfish ambition or vain conceit. Rather, in humility value others above yourselves, not looking to your own interests but each of you to the interests of the others" (Philippians 2:3–4). God is so good to provide correction and refinement for us through his Word.

LORD,

Thank you for your Word and for pursuing me, especially when I am not doing what is right. Your guidance is precious to me and I am grateful for it. Help me to be sensitive to your correction and to repent from my sins quickly. Thank you for Jesus and his example for me. I want to grow to be more like him.

AMEN.

FOR A PURPOSE
AND ON PURPOSE

JOHN 15:16

You did not choose me, but I chose you. I appointed you to go and produce fruit and that your fruit should remain, so that whatever you ask the Father in my name, he will give you.

John 15:16

Do you remember the Old Testament story of Elijah and the widow? You can read more about it in 1 Kings 17:7–16. In a nutshell, God instructed Elijah that when he arrived at a town called Zarephath, he was to go up to a widow there and ask her for some bread. Sure enough, as Elijah walked up to the town, he saw a woman and he called out to her, asking her for a bit of her bread. The widow replied, "I don't have any bread, just a small amount of flour and a bit of oil; it's barely enough for me to make a loaf for my son and me. After I make this little loaf, we are all but dead; I have nothing more." Elijah told the widow to not be afraid and asked her to give him a piece of her bread. Then Elijah told the widow, "The flour in your jar will not become empty and the oil jug will not run dry until the day the

LORD sends rain on the surface of the land." In other words, he told her that God would keep her stocked with food until the drought was over and she could grow food again. The widow did what Elijah instructed and she kept her household—including her houseguest Elijah—well-fed without the flour or oil running out.

Recently I heard a preacher share this story about Elijah. The preacher had a beautiful point: She highlighted that this widow did not tell a lie; she really didn't have any bread to give to Elijah. The widow only had the ingredients to make bread, but she did not have the actual loaf of bread, the end product. It is the same with us. We have the gifts—the ingredients—to be of use to God and do good in this world. But we do not have the end product—the polished, fully put-together offering. God wants you to offer back to him your gifts—your "ingredients"—so that he can use them to make his end product. I love how this preacher summed this story up and applied it to God's people today: "We have been called by God for a purpose and on purpose."

LORD,

Thank you for inviting us to work by your side. Thank you for giving us skills and gifts that we can then offer back to your service. Allow us to grab hold of your invitation to join you in doing your work.

AMEN.

PRAY ALL THE TIME

PHILIPPIANS 4:6–7

Don't worry about anything, but in everything, through prayers and petition with thanksgiving, present your requests to God. And the peace of God, which surpasses all understanding, will guard your hearts and minds in Christ Jesus.

Philippians 4:6–7

On a Sunday in February 2022, I came to church with a heavy heart because of what was happening in Ukraine. Some Ukrainians were waking up to a completely different reality because Russia was attacking them. I did not know all the background to that situation; all I knew was that one country was bombing another and the lives of very real people were in danger. I was stunned into stillness; I felt frozen. I felt hopeless; all I could do was go through the motions of the day.

When I got to church, I started talking to friends. I noticed my young friend Talia's nails: each nail was painted yellow at the base and blue at the tip, like the colors of the Ukrainian flag. Her nails were bright and beautiful and caught my eye quickly. When I asked Talia about them, she told me, "They remind me to pray for Ukraine." She said it so quickly and steadily. In the most respectful way, Talia told me, "Mrs. Des, prayer is powerful."

What struck me was Talia's faith and steadfastness in the Lord. Talia spoke power into me and she probably didn't even know it. She reminded me that God in me is powerful; prayer is key in everything in this life, in all the big and seemingly small matters. Even when I feel like I can do nothing, I can still pray. And if I have to paint my nails to remind myself when my faith starts to wane, then I'll do it! You, too, are stronger than you realize. The little things do matter when they point us back to a big, powerful Father. The weight that I had before church was lifted. I could join my friend and sister Talia by way of prayer.

FATHER GOD,

Thank you for this reminder that you have given me power through prayer. Thank you for the truth in Psalm 145:17–19 (CSB): "The LORD is righteous in all his ways and faithful in all his acts. The LORD is near all who call out to him, all who call out to him with integrity. He fulfills the desire of those who fear him, he hears their cry for help and saves them." I believe this truth and walk in it today.

AMEN.

WORDS OF ENCOURAGEMENT

PROVERBS 3:27

Do not withhold good from those to whom it is due, when it is in your power to act.

Proverbs 3:27

The book of Ruth is an Old Testament book. Typically, when people talk about it, they talk about Ruth's faith and loyalty, but I wanted to highlight Boaz and what it means to speak a blessing over others. In Ruth 2, Naomi—Ruth's mother-in-law—and Ruth have walked all the way back to Bethlehem from Moab. Ruth asks permission to go to a nearby field to collect grain that has fallen on the ground for food from the harvest, and Naomi tells her to go. The nearby field happens to belong to Boaz, a relative of Naomi's. As Ruth is picking up the grain pieces, Boaz notices her and asks about her. He instructs his workers to watch over her, to provide water for her, and to make sure she collects more than enough. Boaz is moved by how Ruth has loved, honored, and cared for Naomi. Boaz is a man who loves the Lord and knows he is loved by the Lord. Overflowing with this love and generosity, he gives Ruth a beautiful blessing: "May the LORD reward you for what you have done, and may you receive a full reward from the LORD God of Israel, under whose wings you have come for refuge" (Ruth 2:12 CSB).

Boaz speaks words of blessing over Ruth. When God gives us words to speak to or over any other human, it is our duty to do it. Not for recognition or praise from others but because it is a good gift that we have been invited to share. Words are powerful and good; loving words from one person to another can do mighty things. When we speak blessings to and over one another, we are following in Jesus's ways.

Jesus,

Thank you for your example and thank you for letting me share in spreading joy and encouragement here on earth. Help me to lovingly share uplifting words to anyone you put in my path. Let me be a person-builder, a cheerleader, and an encourager. Allow me to follow Jesus's command in John 15:12 (CSB): "This is my command: Love one another as I have loved you."

Amen.

Help my unbelief!

HEBREWS 11:1

Now faith is the reality of what is hoped for, the proof of what is not seen.

Hebrews 11:1

When Jesus was here on earth, he only traveled a short distance from where he was born, about 150 miles. Yet he made a huge impact and performed many miracles, including healing people who were sick or disabled. Jesus was a healer, the likes of which this world had never seen. In Mark 9, we find a story of a father who comes to Jesus, looking for healing for his son. The son has an unclean spirit in him that is constantly trying to kill him—throwing the boy into bodies of water to drown him, or into fires to burn him up. Once the boy is in Jesus's presence, the demon throws the boy down to the ground, causing him to convulse and foam from his mouth. The man asked Jesus to help his son, "if you can."

Jesus replies to the man, "'And Jesus said to him, "'If you can'! All things are possible for one who believes." Immediately the father of the child cried out and said, "I believe;

help my unbelief!" (Mark 9:23–24, ESV)
Jesus delights in us telling the truth. He is there when we come to the end of ourselves, realizing that we can't handle things in our own power. Jesus healed the man's son by taking away the evil spirit, and Jesus also healed the father by meeting him where he was, helping him realize that his faith was waning. The father was lacking full belief, and it was almost like he was realizing it out loud while talking to Jesus. Jesus had mercy for the father. God wants to hear our struggles. He wants to hear the potentially shameful and difficult things for us to admit. He wants our honesty because most of all, Jesus wants all of our heart. Nothing can scare God away from us; he already knows everything anyway. We have a standing invitation from God to share every need so that he can take care of them.

ABBA,

Thank you for loving me fully and completely. Thank you for sending Jesus to show me by his example how to live on earth and especially for his sacrifice for me. Allow me to be honest with you about everything that I am dealing with in my life and help me to trust you with the outcome. You have done good things for me and I know you will always take care of me.

AMEN.

BE STILL AND KNOW THAT I AM GOD

PSALM 46:10

Weekly Reflection

NOTES, THOUGHTS, PRAYERS, ETC.

I AM A SERVANT LEADER

JOHN 20:21

Again Jesus said, "Peace be with you! As the Father has sent me, I am sending you."

John 20:21

I have a good friend named Victoria. After COVID-19 came into our lives, God prompted me to ask her to read a book with me. It really didn't make a whole lot of sense to me at the time, since we were still in a pandemic and trying to be careful.

We decided to meet in our backyards one evening a week with our masks on. When we started, I didn't even have any idea what book I would suggest for us. But our two-woman book club quickly turned into a gaggle of girls, and we now have anywhere from thirteen to fifteen ladies coming each week. We are currently reading our fourth book.

One evening, Victoria was sharing a revelation with our group. She told us how, when the group started, she was talking to her husband about being asked to be a leader in the group. She asked for time to think about it and came home to talk it over with her husband. She told him, "I should probably pray about it and see what God says." Victoria's husband responded, "Why do you have to pray about it? You already know the answer! God set you in this Bible study, he already gave you permission, and you're supposed to serve him when you are asked!"

We do this a lot, don't we? We forget that we have already been sent and are already on mission. Even if we don't feel prepared, ready, or equipped, the good news is that we don't have to be. We just have to say "yes" to God and allow him to set the rest up for us. I remember a few times when I was so scared that I turned down requests to help or lead. But I also recognize that God did not give up on me, because he kept coming after me with more offers to help and lead, joining him in kingdom-building work. He does not give up on us. Maybe you are involved in a group right now where you are a brilliant beam of light, and maybe God will invite you into opportunities to help there. Don't be shy; do not doubt yourself or God; do not fear or try to postpone. You were called there for that moment. Stand up and take the invitation that your heavenly Father is giving you!

Father in Heaven,

When you present an opportunity for me to serve, be it a leadership position or something else, give me boldness to say "yes" and to serve. Help me to give everything I have to you and your children. Use me mightily, Lord God.

Amen.

YOU ARE QUALIFIED

2 CORINTHIANS 3:5

Not that we are competent in ourselves to claim anything for ourselves, but our competence comes from God.

2 Corinthians 3:5

My daughters and I are reading the New Testament together and I can still remember the day we started Matthew, which starts like this: "An account of the genealogy of Jesus Christ, the Son of David, the Son of Abraham." I thought, "Oh no. Can't I just skip this chapter, God? All I am going to do is stumble over these hard-to-pronounce names and it's just a list. Is it really that important?"

He didn't answer me directly, but I began to read anyway and as I read that long list of hard-to-pronounce names, I started to feel great comfort. Those names in that long list mean something and are vital to me, just like any parable, proverb, psalm, or story, because it too is helpful information. We see that Jesus has an extensive earthly family and that he has some notably famous people in his lineage. We see four women named among all of the references to "this man fathered this man." In a time when women weren't counted as significant, there are four times when we read "this man fathered a man by a woman." Rahab was the first, Ruth is immediately after, Bathsheba is two sons later, and finally Mary concludes Jesus's family tree.

Each of these women was not only a second-class citizen in their time because of their gender, but they were also "not the right kind of woman." Rahab was a prostitute, a dishonorable occupation. Ruth was from Moab, a nation that was an enemy of Israel. Bathsheba was an already married woman waiting for her warrior husband to come home and who was taken as girlfriend by King David, and Mary was an ordinary teenage girl from Nazareth, a city that was not well regarded.

Jesus's lineage is full of brokenness and shameful stories, but we see through Jesus's example that bad decisions, lowly societal placement, or sin in your family story does not disqualify you from showing up and serving God right where you are. Perhaps author Rachel Held Evans said it best: "Because even God was born into a dysfunctional family of faith, and did not wait around for ideal conditions before showing up." This is true for believers today, this is true for you, friend; no matter your gender, your age, or where you come from. If you believe in Jesus, you can serve God and He wants you.

LORD,

I praise you that I do not have to be perfect or qualified to belong to you and to work for you. Thank you for welcoming me into your family with my flaws and all. Let me remember this truth and strengthen me from attacks that try to tell me that I am not worthy. I am made worthy because of Jesus.

AMEN.

No Retirement in the Kingdom of Heaven

PHILIPPIANS 1:6

I am sure of this, that he who started a good work in you will carry it on to completion until the day of Christ Jesus.

Philippians 1:6

In Luke 2:36, we meet an old woman named Anna. She is a widow, meaning that she was once married, but her husband passed away when she was young. This loss for Anna did not disturb her faith in God. In fact, she drew nearer to God, and gave the rest of her life to God and the people of God. Anna fasted and prayed all day long in the temple. She was patiently waiting for the promised Messiah to come. She knew the promises and stories of the Bible and she knew the prophecies that God had spoken and would fulfill.

Anna was a prophet herself and she was a living example of what my wise friend, Mitzi, told me recently: "There is no retirement in the Kingdom of God." After many years of serving God, Anna was one of the first two people in the temple to see the baby Jesus come in with his parents, to be consecrated as the Jewish law required. Anna recognized him immediately and proclaimed Jesus as the Savior for all who would listen, that this baby was the Messiah, the one whom they had been waiting for to redeem God's people. Scholars debate that at this time Anna of Asher might have been anywhere from 84 to 104. Anna was elderly and she was still serving God. Anna didn't worry about putting her feet up, taking care of herself, maintaining things of her own, or feeding herself. Anna's focus was doing what God was asking her to do. For Anna, that meant being in the temple day and night, Scripture says, and fasting and praying for the people in her community. Anna was—and still is today—an example of God's good work.

GOD,

Your direction for each of our lives looks different, wherever you take us, whatever you give us. May we follow only you and may we not look to a time of retirement but to always find joy and fulfillment in serving you here until you call us home. Give us endurance and perseverance to run the race you have set before each of us, and to do it well.

AMEN.

WHAT'S RIGHT

ROMANS 12:1-2

Therefore, brothers and sisters, in view of the mercies of God, I urge you to present your bodies as a living sacrifice, holy and pleasing to God; this is your true worship. Do not be conformed to this age, but be transformed by the renewing of your mind, so that you may discern what is the good, pleasing and perfect will of God.

Romans 12:1-2

Standing up for what is right can be extremely difficult. I never want to be the odd girl out. Even when I strongly disagree with what people are saying, I do not want to share what I am thinking. Recently I revisited a book about a brave, God-loving man named Dietrich Bonhoeffer. Dietrich was a young German man who studied theology and he loved to talk about God and people with anyone who would listen. He was from a large family and they lived through both World War I and World War II. Dietrich was able to listen and watch when Adolf Hitler and the German Socialist Party rose to power as World War II began. Dietrich was one of the first in

Europe to see what Hitler was stirring up, and he spoke up against the mistreatment of the Jewish people. Dietrich was a believer of Jesus. He was not Jewish, but he was a firm believer that hatred of a people group was not Christlike and was wrong. Dietrich told anyone who listened and beckoned his German community to listen to him and to join him in standing against what Hitler and the German Socialist party were doing. A few people listened, but the majority did not. Dietrich became a target of Adolf Hitler, who eventually had Dietrich arrested, held in a prison, then sent to concentration camps, and finally executed. Hitler did all of this because Dietrich believed in Jesus, lived like God directed him, and spoke up when others were being mistreated. Dietrich became an enemy of the German government because of his relationship with God, and he chose God over his personal well being. Dietrich gave up his comfort and convenience in order to help people that he had no direct connection with other than recognizing the wrong instigated against them. Dietrich is one example of a person who chose the way of Jesus. May we be women of God ready to stand up and use whatever we have to follow Jesus's example, just like Dietrich did.

LORD OF ALL,

Thank you for protecting me and helping me during big, difficult, life-altering situations, and during small, everyday challenges. Be with me, Abba, and give me courage and strength when you call me to stand up for what is right, even if others want to do the wrong thing. Grow my integrity and character to look more like your Son, Jesus.

AMEN.

DAY 20

GOD IS OUR COMFORT AND STRENGTH

PSALM 34:18

The LORD is close to the brokenhearted and saves those who are crushed in spirit.

Psalm 34:18

The world is a tough place, with many disappointments, difficulties, and stresses. At times in our lives, it can feel like wave after powerful wave knocking us over, water rushing into our eyes and noses, making it difficult to do anything else except try and breathe and get ourselves up and out of the way. It would be completely understandable to want to get angry, frustrated, and resentful and allow the spirit of bitterness to take over us. Just recently my family experienced a loss of a family member and our lives are forever altered by their absence. We rejoice that this person is in heaven, but we mourn that they are no longer with us. Sometimes the pain of the loss produces endless streams of tears and deep longing to see the person's face, hear their voice, or receive a hug from them. It's hard to fully explain, but sometimes I felt a consistent presence that held me tight and gave me strength that I couldn't identify in the moment, when my feelings were overwhelming. But as I reflect back on those moments, I see that Psalm 34:18 explains what I was experiencing: God was that comfort and strength. Even when we are distracted by temporary frustration, anger, loss, or pain, God is near and desires to comfort us with his steadfast truth. He is always with us; he loves us and he provides for everything we need. May we be people who always look for God and his provision, because he is there—even in our darkest moments. Let us commit to memory and believe: "The LORD himself goes before you and will be with you; he will never leave you nor forsake you. Do not be afraid; do not be discouraged." — Deuteronomy 31:8

ABBA,

Thank you for your steadfast love and care. I don't understand why tough things happen to me or to those I love, but I know that you are good, you love me, and you are with me. Help me to not need reasons or explanations but to just believe you and trust you. When you do give me answers, help me to praise you for your generosity. I praise you when I can stay obedient amidst great adversity and when I fail; I praise you that you give me second chances. Thank you for never leaving me and for being with me when I am brokenhearted and crushed in spirit.

AMEN.

YOUR WORD IS A LAMP FOR MY FEET

A LIGHT ON MY PATH

PSALM
119:105

Weekly Reflection

Be the Solution

ROMANS 15:13

May the God of hope fill you with all joy and peace as you trust in him, so that you may overflow with hope by the power of the Holy Spirit.

Romans 15:13

I have a friend who used to live in a neighborhood with a park that had a basketball court, and the neighborhood kids would play pickup basketball games every day. We live in south Texas and these basketball players would get super thirsty as they played under the hot Texas sun. The only water fountain was in a gated part of the park, and many of the kids did not have access to it. The kids would end up jumping the gate to get a drink and the neighborhood board did not like this at all. My friend's neighborhood was in an uproar, and pretty soon, two camps emerged over how to handle the situation. One group thought that the neighborhood needed to build a water fountain outside of the gate so that the players could have water to drink, and the other group thought that the kids needed to plan ahead and demonstrate personal responsibility by bringing their own water. But then there was one neighbor who took that responsibility on himself. He installed a water fountain in his front yard so that anyone, especially the basketball players, could have cold drinks of fresh water. Instead of joining in the chorus of complaints or sitting in frustration, he decided to help. This neighbor bought the components and committed the resources for a solution. This neighbor's kindness and generous act led the way for others to be kind and generous, too.

I have heard it said that if you're being critical of something a brother or sister in Christ—or anyone for that matter—is doing, then you are not helpful to or supportive of them. I was so encouraged by this neighbor who built the water fountain because he was showing us the incarnate way, the way of Jesus. When there is a problem, I don't want to look for someone to blame or allow my imagination to run wild with worst-case scenarios; I want to be moved to actions that overflow out of love. I want to be a helper and contribute to a solution. I don't know if this neighbor knew who Jesus was, but he sure was acting like Jesus.

LORD,

I am so grateful for your Son Jesus and his example of how to live. Strengthen me to be a helper to people in my life and protect me from worry and fear, because nothing good comes from either of those feelings. Thank you for giving me the capacity to be a problem-solver and peacemaker. Bless me with courage to follow you when difficult situations arise in my life.

AMEN.

NO SCARCITY WITH GOD

2 CORINTHIANS 9:8

And God is able to bless you abundantly, so that in all things at all times, having all that you need, you will abound in every good work.

2 Corinthians 9:8

When you are surrounded by other believers who love and seek the Lord daily, a by-product is that you will constantly be learning from them. Your friends will share so many wonderful thoughts, perspectives, prayers, and theology that will point you to Jesus and strengthen your relationship with God. I once had a conversation with a friend who shared this idea of scarcity—the state of being in short supply. What happens to you when you feel like something that you need or want is in threat of being in short supply? I realized that I would more than likely panic and flail. I could see myself thinking of the worst-case scenario and coming up with actionable ways to take care of myself. I would develop a "survival of the fittest" mindset; I would become an "only the strong will survive" kind of person. But this way of acting is the opposite of how Christ

Jesus has instructed us to think, act, and live, and it is born out of our human weakness. There's only thirty minutes of hot water in the campground showers. Only four muffins for breakfast tomorrow, one soda left, one set of sunglasses, one last seat on the bus. When I allow this feeling of scarcity to take hold of me, I stop seeing others as important. All I see is my need and myself. Everything that Jesus taught about loving, considering, and taking care of others flies out of the window when scarcity takes hold. But what a great Father we have, that he doesn't let us go. He is not angry with us; he reaches out to us with merciful correction, gracious forgiveness, and generous reminders. Even when, like selfish children, we try to hoard stuff for ourselves, he wants to guide us back to the truth that we have all that we need and he will completely provide.

LORD,

When I am tempted to believe that there's not enough, will you guide me back to your truths? Remind me that you will always take care of every need, so I don't need to worry or fight to get my needs covered. Please forgive me if I have mistreated another person when I have felt scarcity and allow me to learn from my mistake and grow to be more like Jesus

AMEN.

Second chances

MATTHEW 6:24

No one can serve two masters. Either you will hate the one and love the other, or you will be devoted to the one and despise the other. You cannot serve both God and money.

Matthew 6:24

Two men came to the cross to bring down Jesus's body after he was crucified: Joseph of Arimathea, and Nicodemus (You can read this story in Luke 19:38-42). They were both men of means, well known and influential at the time that Jesus lived on earth. They both talked with Jesus, but neither of them were willing to damage their reputations or livelihoods in order to actively follow Jesus before his death on the cross. However, our God is a God of second chances and he is all about pursuing us because his desire is to redeem us and pull us back close to him. God was not done with Nicodemus and Joseph. These two men did answer God's call, and after Jesus was crucified, they used their status in the community to pull strings in order to get Jesus's body down from the cross—a remarkable feat in an era when the

Roman officials would have typically left the condemned person's body as a warning for others. After Joseph and Nicodemus got permission, they did the physical labor of removing Jesus's body from the cross, transporting his body to Joseph's tomb, and cleansing and preparing it with spices and linen.

What Joseph and Nicodemus failed to do when Jesus was alive, they succeeded in doing after his death. They said "yes" to the second invitation to follow and serve Jesus. They fully put their lives in God's hands, and gave up their cushy comfort and reliable worldly wealth to serve Jesus. Where is God calling you to serve him? Where have you been telling God "no" or "hold on, I don't want to do that just yet." You can obey right now, repent from your disobedience, ask for forgiveness, and do what he has been asking you to do.

FATHER,

You are patient, persistent, and kind to me. Forgive me for wanting to take care of myself instead of doing what you have asked me to do. Give me courage and make me able to do whatever you ask me to do. I am grateful you are my Heavenly Father. Thank you for your mercy.

AMEN.

A HAPPY ENDING

DANIEL 10:19

And he said, "O man greatly loved, fear not, peace be with you; be strong and of good courage." And as he spoke to me, I was strengthened and said, "Let my lord speak, for you have strengthened me."

Daniel 10:19

I was struck after reading in the Gospels that there were times when Jesus was almost killed while ministering but he showed his power by safely and calmly walking away from the danger. In Luke 4:29–30 and in John 8:58–59, we read that Jesus was preaching and the people who were there either wanted to throw him off of a cliff or stone him to death. But both times Jesus simply walked away. John 8:59 says Jesus "slipped away" and Luke 4:30 says, "But he walked right through the crowd and went on his way." Jesus was a man and I bet he picked up on the tension, anger, and violence that was coursing through the people standing before him. But he was also equally God and he knew it was not his time yet, and so he walked on his way in those two instances. Jesus still had work to do for his Father and his end was coming, but it wouldn't be off the side of the cliff or by stones being hurled at him … it would actually be a lot worse and Jesus knew exactly how.

I'm reminded of a story a pastor once told me about a superhero TV show. In one particular episode, the superheroes are about to fight with the bad guys, but before the fight starts, they are stopped by a vision of themselves fighting and winning against these significantly bigger enemies. But they noticed that in this vision, they are all wearing different clothes; clothes that they had never seen before, not the clothes they had on right then, but new clothes. They realize that they make it to the next day, that they will win the battle they are about to enter, so they approach that day's battle like they have nothing to lose, because they don't! They had the privilege of seeing that glimpse of their future, and so they give it all they have and fight like they have nothing to lose! They give all of their skill, energy, and power and they whip the bad guys and are triumphant.

What if this is how God wants us to live? Like the example Jesus showed in the accounts of Luke and John, he has already told us that as his children, we each have a happy ending of eternity with him.

ABBA,

Bless me with your assurance that I belong to you. Thank you for the gifts that you have given me and the tasks that you have invited me into. Allow me to give each day all I have—all my love, mercy, generosity, grace, and forgiveness—knowing that I stand in the security that Jesus gifted me. Help me act more and more like Jesus.

AMEN.

EZER: STRONG RESCUER

2 CORINTHIANS 13:11

Finally, brothers and sisters, rejoice! Strive for full restoration, encourage one another, be of one mind, live in peace. And the God of love and peace will be with you.

2 Corinthians 13:11

You, dear reader, were created as an ezer. *Ezer* is a Hebrew word that means "helper," and it was first used in Genesis 2:18 to describe the first woman that God created, Eve. *Ezer* is also used throughout the Bible to describe God as our helper; it could be translated as "strong rescuer." This makes perfect sense because we as his children are made in his image and are to mimic his ways. Despite what the world says a helper is—someone who is inferior, a lowly subservient servant—God defines ezer as a rescuer, protector, helper, and equal. God made Eve for Adam to serve with him by his side. Eve was not Adam's subordinate; she was not less than him. Rather, they were equal and they needed each other. Adam and Eve are examples of how God intended for men and women to complement each other. We see other times throughout the Bible where men and women were placed together to help each other do God's work. Priscilla and Aquila were a married couple who led house churches alongside the apostle Paul. Anna and Simeon were the two prophets who met the baby Jesus in the Jerusalem temple, recognized him, and proclaimed and blessed him. Mary and Joseph, Jesus's parents, were both needed to raise Jesus here on earth together. Ruth and Boaz were paired together to continue to build Jesus's lineage.

These men and women "teams" were meant to do their work together, complementing each other, working side by side, and making one another stronger in their tasks. We are each called to be *ezers*: helpers, rescuers, and protectors. There's plenty of work to be done if we look around us and follow God as he reveals what he needs for us to do.

LORD GOD,

Thank you for loving me and enabling me to be a strong helper. Thank you for Jesus and his example for me to follow. Lord, strengthen me to fully walk in my strong helper identity and obey you when you instruct me to help. Allow me to be a supportive teammate to whomever you place in my path and work hard because I am working for you and your glory.

AMEN.

Weekly Reflection

DAY 26

GENEROUS BLESSING

PHILIPPIANS 2:3–4

Do nothing out of selfish ambition or vain conceit. Rather, in humility value others above yourselves, not looking to your own interests but each of you to the interests of the others.

Philippians 2:3–4

Have you ever watched a video on the internet where one person is blessing another person? Maybe they are fulfilling a wish list for the other person, or maybe they see that one person is in need of a particular item. Whatever the need may be, someone is coming along and providing for another.

Sometimes these two people are strangers to one another, at other times they may be acquaintances, friends, or family surprising a loved one. Either way, these videos make my heart flutter and always make me cry tears of joy. One man I follow on Instagram has a ton of followers who donate money to him so that he can help people experiencing homelessness in Los Angeles. He befriended many of these people and he drives around checking in on them and making sure they are doing okay. He will ask them, "What do you need right now?" and they'll say stuff like, "I could use a hot meal, a sleeping bag, and some toilet paper." The man will go and gather the items they asked for and then bless the person with more. The homeless person doesn't expect that kindness and inevitably starts crying. To watch someone be blessed with kindness when they might be typically met with the opposite on a daily basis is a generous reminder of the world's need for Jesus's gentle generosity.

When I am able to witness such generosity and Jesus-like love in action, it reminds me of the gentleness that overflows through us from the Holy Spirit. Gentleness is a fruit of the Spirit that Paul describes in Galatians 5:22–23. Gentleness calls us to be teachable, have a humble heart posture, and to not demand our own rights or preferences be upheld, but consider others before ourselves.

When I watch one of those "blessing" videos online, I am reminded that this is what God is calling me to do: to look out for others. Do they have a need? Are they lacking something that I can help with? Is there a kind word that I could speak, an encouragement? Can I offer a cool drink? Would it disrupt my schedule for the day? Would it cost me something financially? Yes, probably. But that is what living in the fruit of gentleness is—being teachable with that humble heart posture and the everyday awareness of others and putting their needs in front of my own. Serving others won't

always be a big action; it could be something small and that is the adventure portion of it. Serving others will be different every time; you have to be willing and open to let God use you where the need is.

LORD,

May I have a teachable heart every day. May I receive your sight to see those around me who may have a need, and may I be moved to action by your love in me. Let me keep my eyes only on you and not get distracted by what others are doing. Help me focus on only what you have gifted and called me to do. I love you, God.

AMEN.

WOMEN OF VALOR

1 SAMUEL 16:7

But the LORD said to Samuel, 'Do not look on his appearance or on the height of his stature, because I have rejected him. For the LORD sees not as man sees: man looks on the outward appearance, but the LORD looks on the heart.'

1 Samuel 16:7

Ruth was a woman of noble character, a woman of valor. In the book of Ruth, we see that her actions to secure her future and provide for her family took bravery, determination, and strength. Ruth remained loyal to her mother-in-law, Naomi, even when Naomi told her multiple times to go back to her own parents. Ruth showed how strong she was to move to Israel, where she was not liked, and demonstrated bold determination when she went out alone to collect wheat from Boaz's field. For most of us, our lives are not as challenging as Ruth's, but we still have our daily demands, and they do not lessen our valor. Did you complete the chores your parents assigned you today? Did you say a nice word to your sibling? Did you finish your piano practice? Did you use your best manners when replying to your neighbor on the way to your car? All of these seeming little moments of action are "woman of valor" moments. They are worthy of celebration because it takes courage, boldness, and strength to do them. There will be more significant moments in your day when you will show up as a woman of valor, but big or small moments, they all count! You are a woman of valor, and success or failure, God delights in you!

GOD,

Thank you for pursuing me and helping me become a more whole person. Thank you for never letting me go and for wanting the best for me. Forgive me for the times when I run away from the challenging tasks of the day that you place in front of me. Give me courage and boldness to receive the tasks and please strengthen me to accomplish them, even if at first I may fail. You are the most loving God, who will allow me another chance to try. Thank you, Abba.

AMEN.

PRUNING, IT'S HARD

JOHN 15:1–2

I am the true vine, and my Father is the gardener. He cuts off every branch in me that bears no fruit, while every branch that does bear fruit he prunes so that it will be even more fruitful.

John 15:1–2

I try to grow a garden every spring and summer. I pick the seeds, order them, and map them out nice and orderly. The fun, messy part comes when I get to till the ground and create the rows for their assigned veggies; then I water, watch for growth, and pray that this south Texas sun doesn't scorch the tiny seedlings. The growth is exciting, but also a little bit stressful for me because I am not good at pruning. I want my plants to grow wild and free with essentially no interference from me. What I am learning from my hands-on science experiment is something that God has already spoken about through Jesus: Pruning is necessary and it is good, not just for plants, but for his children, too. My reluctance to prune my plants revealed to me my human weakness and highlighted how much wiser and better God is at caring for his creation than I am. In John 15, the original Greek translation of "prune" in verse 2 means "to clean." Even though it's a tough thing to do, God knows that we need pruning and cleaning so that we can grow stronger and produce more goodness for him. The process is difficult and can be uncomfortable and at times painful, but so very necessary so that we can grow wiser, stronger, and better. I haven't come close to getting better at pruning my own garden—it still grows wild—but I have started watching videos of how to trim some of my specific plants. What I have learned is that different plants need to be trimmed in different ways, and reminds me of how our omniscient God cares for each of his children. If certain plants aren't pruned, they might not be able to yield crops at all, or can only produce a small amount of fruit. If the stems and leaves of a plant are overgrown, water can't go to the important places it's needed, like the blooms where the fruit will come from. Then I've grown a big bush instead of, say, a cucumber plant. Pruning is so important, equal to water and sun so that fruit will be produced. Thank goodness we belong to a wise and loving Father who knows exactly how to help us grow.

LORD,

Thank you for taking such great care of me. Thank you for pursuing me. Help me to seek your pruning because I am never done growing and I know I have a lot to learn. Give me endurance and perseverance to stay the course with your corrections and loving hand.

AMEN.

Forgiveness

COLOSSIANS 3:13

Bear with each other and forgive one another if any of you has a grievance against someone. Forgive as the Lord forgave you.

Colossians 3:13

Forgiveness is tough. When someone hurts you physically or causes harm to you emotionally, it can be difficult to forgive them. I want justice and restitution immediately but that rarely happens. Yet God tells me to forgive even when the person who has hurt me hasn't even asked to be forgiven. I am reminded of the book of Philemon, an extraordinary story of a wealthy man from Colossae named Philemon, the apostle Paul, and another man named Onesimus.

Onesimus was a slave to Philemon, and the text implies that he may have wronged Philemon somehow, so he ran away to Rome. While he was there, he became a follower of Jesus and helped Paul, who was imprisoned in Rome. In fact, they worked so closely together that Onesimus became like a son to Paul. Eventually, Paul needed Onesimus to return to Colossae to help the church there. But there's a problem: Philemon and Onesimus had some unfinished business between them because of the wrong that Onesimus has perpetrated on Philemon. Paul wrote a letter to Philemon before sending Onesimus, asking Philemon to forgive Onesimus and to receive him as a brother because he is now a child of God, a co-heir with Jesus, and therefore a brother in God's adoptive family. Furthermore, Paul says he will pay for any debt Onesimus incurred against Philemon.

What's wild is that Onesimus is a Greek name that means "useful." Paul told Philemon that Onesimus may have once been useless but now his life has been preserved. He has been transformed and become more than useful; Onesimus was restored.

I used to read this story, unable to shake the unfairness of it; I was hyper-focused on justice for Philemon. I totally missed how God was working. Paul, by God's guidance, was offering this upside-down situation to Philemon—to forgive Onesimus for whatever he had done, to forget the cultural norms of the time, and to see him as an equal, instead of the enslaved man that he was. The focus was not on what Philemon lost and whatever hurt Onesimus might have inflicted on Philemon. Instead, the aim of Paul's letter was to lift Philemon's eyes back to Jesus and what was important: Onesimus's salvation and forgiveness. Paul wasn't trying to make

light of what Onesimus had done or take anything away from Philemon. He wanted to point Philemon to the grander picture of the many thousands of people throughout the Roman empire being saved and that included Onesimus. For Philemon to extend forgiveness and work as equals with Onesimus was to be doing God's work and to be living like Jesus.

LORD,

You know I am weak at times and I want to fight to get justice for myself. Help me, Father, to be about your work and trust that you have me completely covered with all of my physical, emotional, and spiritual needs. If there is a person that I need to seek reconciliation with, will you bring them to my mind? If I have done something wrong, will you remind me so that I can take responsibility for it and seek to restore the wrong that I have done? Thank you for loving me and pursuing me, and for helping me grow healthy and strong.

AMEN.

CHILDREN OF GOD

ISAIAH 41:10

So do not fear, for I am with you; do not be dismayed, for I am your God. I will strengthen you and help you; I will uphold you with my righteous right hand.

Isaiah 41:10

Habakkuk was an Old Testament prophet, but he wasn't a typical prophet because he didn't use his prophetic gifting to warn the people of Israel. Instead, Habakkuk spoke with God about what he saw the people of Israel doing and shared his struggles and complaints about how they were acting. What I appreciate the most about Habakkuk is how he interacted with God. Habakkuk lived into his relationship with God just like a true son. The book of Habakkuk is a wonderful example for us to observe and learn from because it shows how God truly sees us—he is not afraid of our questions, our complaints, or our struggles. God welcomes it all. These types of interactions with God deepen our relationship with him, and he desires to help us in every aspect of our lives. Sometimes he will give us answers, though they may not always be what we want to hear or walk through. Sometimes God may not explain what he is doing, and it may even seem like God is ignoring us altogether. But we know because of how God has shown up throughout the Bible, as well as in our lives, that no matter what, he will not leave us or forsake us.

God gave Habakkuk answers to his complaints and then asked him to record a vision that was going to happen at God's appointed time. Habakkuk encourages me to bring my true self to my relationship with God, to share my genuine thoughts, fears, and frustrations with him, knowing that he is listening with love to me. I have this false idea that I can offend God or anger him if I share anything that isn't happy or good. But if God is in pursuit of our hearts, then he wants our genuine selves, not a false self or some version of ourselves we think pleases God. We already please him more than we can know and he already knows all my thoughts. So he knows when I'm frustrated with my sister, angry at my parents, and ignoring my best friend. God asks us to be truthful with him. He wants to be invited into these struggles with us, not so he can lecture us but so that he can listen to what we are going through and then show us his might. "Cast all your anxiety on him because he cares for you" (1 Peter 5:7). That's how God's relationship was with Habakkuk all the way back then, and that is what he invites us into today.

LORD GOD,

I am sorry for thinking that I need to present a perfect and clean version of myself to you. First of all, there is no such thing because I am constantly sinning; and secondly, you desire truth from me—you desire a real relationship with me and for true growth to happen in me. Help me to boldly share my true self and trust that you will heal me and help me grow in maturity. Thank you for loving me all the days of my life and for welcoming me into your family. Thank you for not letting me go and for caring for me, even when I am choosing the wrong path. I love you.

AMEN.

ENCOURAGE ONE ANOTHER

&

BUILD EACH OTHER UP

1 THESSALONIANS 5:11

Weekly Reflection

_____

_____

_____

_____

_____

_____

_____

_____

_____

_____

_____

_____

_____

_____

_____

_____

_____

_____

_____

_____

_____

_____

NOTES, THOUGHTS, PRAYERS, ETC.

PERFECTLY TIMED BLESSINGS

MATTHEW 6:25, 30

This is why I tell you to never be worried about your life, for all that you need will be provided, such as food, water, clothing—everything your body needs. Isn't there more to your life than a meal? Isn't your body more than clothing? ....
So if God has clothed the meadow with hay, which is here for such a short time and then dried up and burned, won't he provide for you the clothes you need—you of little faith?

Matthew 6:25, 30

My family and I have needed a bigger car for a long time—one with more than five seats, super cold air conditioning, a back-up camera, and a sunroof. But as we prayed for God's guidance on this matter, it felt like he was quiet. Then one day, a couple from our church offered us their car for free. They had just bought a newer car and had no need for an extra vehicle that still ran great, so they asked if we wanted it. They had no idea that we were in need. It was amazing to watch how God answered our prayers through someone else's action. We now had this free car that could fit our family, had a working air conditioner, and ran great. We praised God for this provision, and every time we got into the car I would praise him for his goodness.

However, our oldest daughter had to sit in the middle of the back seat with her knees scrunched up to her chin—so I still brought my desire to have a bigger car so that we could all fit in comfortably. One particular summer Saturday evening, our family had taken some time to pray for God to provide a bigger car for us. The next day, my brother-in-law and his family came over for a surprise visit with us—which was delightful in itself and made even sweeter when, as they left, my brother-in-law tossed my husband a pair of keys and told us that we could borrow their extra car for as long as we needed it. God heard our prayers and he provided! The second car was a two-door Mini Cooper, a super cool-looking car that could go really fast, but it only fit four people. Our family couldn't help but laugh because we saw how God was providing for us, and we were forced to see that although we didn't understand his blessing right then, we recognized and trusted that he knew what he was doing. What he gave us was exactly what we needed, because that is the kind of Father he is. As the year progressed, we had ups and downs with the cars, but God remained faithful and provided more free cars for us from generous brothers and sisters in our community. It has been amazing to reflect on how God provided through his people. None of the cars were my dream car, but they were each a blessing to my family and me. They were the perfect fit for the time we were able to use them, and not only did our family directly experience God's generosity and provision, but our community got to witness God's faithfulness and provision through our need.

LORD,

Thank you for taking care of every need, little and big, significant and seemingly insignificant. Thank you for loving me so well even when your answers don't make sense to me. Thank you for providing them anyway and revealing yourself in your perfect timing. Help me to continue to have a heart of gratitude to you, Father.

AMEN.

SLOW TO ANGER

JAMES 1:19

My dearest brothers and sisters, take this to heart: Be quick to listen, but slow to speak. And be slow to become angry.

James 1:19

A good friend of mine was sharing with me that her family had been going through some tough things for quite a while. Almost a year before that, though, God gave her this Scripture from James, one that we need every single second of every single day, even if everything is going great in our lives. My friend gratefully received the truth in James 1:9 and went along her way. A year later, she was in the middle of division in her family—her parents were on the brink of possibly divorcing and her siblings were caught in the middle of it, each responding in different ways. But God had given her this Scripture from James to cling to and it set her feet on his firm foundation and allowed her to walk with love and compassion. My friend still has times when she cries, and feels the pain of the division and the stress of her situation, particularly during the holidays. She still gets her feelings hurt, still sometimes hears a harsh word spoken to her, or an accusation thrown at her. But when those things happen, she remembers James 1:9 and is brought back to focus on Jesus.

She is fully leaning into God and is constantly comforted by the God of the universe. Even when things are upended and feel hopeless, she is strong because she believes that God will handle it. She is obeying his instructions so that she can be used for good both within her family and outside of it, in her community.

My friend reminds me of the apostle Paul as he traveled to different regions and ministered to people, sharing the good news of the gospel. Paul was often met with opposition and often thrown into jail. Paul did not resist; he did not physically fight nor did he get angry at those who did or said harmful things to him. He desired what Jesus desires, for all to listen to his words, believe the truth, and be a part of God's family. Read through the book of Acts and see how Paul was the consummate listener and always filled with compassion; the only anger he showed was righteous anger.

LORD GOD,

You are the best at providing for my needs before I even know that I am in need. Continue to grow me in your wisdom and love so that I can be quick to listen and slow to speak and slow to become angry. I desire to serve you like Jesus did and be an agent of change for your glory. Thank you for loving me.

AMEN.

GOD AS OUR LEADER

PSALM 34:4

I sought the LORD, and he answered me; he delivered me from all my fears.

Psalm 34:4

Three of the four gospels record a story of a woman whom Jesus heals. The woman had a bleeding disorder, and had basically been on her monthly cycle for twelve years straight. She had been to many doctors to try and find healing from her affliction, but she had found no relief. Then one day the woman joined a crowd of people around Jesus as he was on his way to heal a little girl. Out of desperation and faith, the woman reached out and touched part of Jesus's cloak. The Bible says that immediately the woman was healed. Jesus felt the power go out from him and he stopped walking and asked the crowd who touched his clothes. The woman, realizing that she had been healed, spoke up and threw herself down at his feet. Jesus did not scold her; instead, he proclaimed her faith in the middle of that large crowd and that she should go in peace and be free from her suffering (you can read more about this in Matthew 9, Mark 5, and

Luke 8).

Many times in my life, I have tried to do things on my own, tried to find solutions to the situations and problems that came my way. But when I finally came to the end of what I could do, at the end of my maneuvers and my possible solutions was God. He was waiting for me with an invitation to rest, to rely on him, and put my faith fully in his plan. His results varied from what I had wanted to not at all what I was thinking, and regardless, God's way was the best way. How many times have we stubbornly tried to have our way, knowing full well that God was waiting patiently to help us? May we continue to grow in maturity to be quicker to allow God to take the lead throughout our lives and guide us in his way. "You who fear him, trust in the LORD—he is their help and shield" (Psalm 115:11).

FATHER,

Thank you for being a perfect leader and Father to me. Thank you for your generous mercy that you show me. Help me to grow in maturity in my faith so that I may more quickly allow you to lead me in the challenges and situations of each day.

AMEN.

SHOOTING STARS

LUKE 12: 22, 29, 31–32

Then he said to his disciples, 'Therefore I tell you, don't worry about your life, what you will eat; or about the body, what you will wear…Don't strive for what you should eat and what you should drink, and don't be anxious…But seek his kingdom, and these things will be provided for you. Don't be afraid, little flock, because your Father delights to give you the kingdom'.

Luke 12: 22, 29, 31–32

One thing to know about my husband Erastos is that he loves stars. All throughout our dating relationship, this guy has always been on the lookout for shooting stars. We spent tons of time in the evenings outside, battling mosquitoes just to catch a glimpse of one star flying above us. Shooting stars are meaningful to him, and to our relationship.

I was diagnosed with Type 1 Diabetes in the fall of 2008, when I was about to become a first-time mama. I was so scared and I had no idea what diabetes was, exactly, so I had no idea how to take care of myself.

It's wonderful to be able to look back and remember the steps that I have taken with this illness and to see how God was providing absolutely everything that I needed. On the afternoon that my body broke down due to my blood sugars being too high for too long, Erastos was at home with me. We were admitted to the hospital that evening and Erastos had to make a trip back to our house to pick up the things we would need to sleep over at the hospital. As he was walking to our car with our bag, he prayed through worried tears that God would protect and take care of our baby and me. As he looked up to the night sky, the brightest shooting star flew across the sky right above him. When he returned to the hospital, he came into our room, dropped our bag, and collapsed into my lap. He sobbed as he told me what he had seen and how he felt God answered him, and gave him reassurance that God was going to take care of me, our baby, and every need—great or small.

God is faithful and tells the truth: Our baby girl Olivia was born healthy and perfect, and my diabetic supplies were completely provided for—and they still are to this day. Diabetes is an expensive illness. God's provision for his people is real, perfect, and complete; he does not fail us, and he will not forget us. And sometimes if we are paying close attention, we can see God showing us that he is near to us, reassuring us of his promises and answering our prayers in his way.

LORD GOD,

You are so good all of the time. Even when I don't get the answer that I want or according to my timing, I know that you are still good. Thank you for being a good and faithful Father to me. You provide all good things for me. You delight in me and I belong to you. Thank you for loving me, Abba.

AMEN.

SPURRING EACH OTHER ON

HEBREWS 10:24–25

And let us consider how we may spur one another on toward love and good deeds, not giving up meeting together, as some are in the habit of doing, but encouraging one another—and all the more as you see the Day approaching.

Hebrews 10:24–25

Have you ever had a friend who always seems to be able to encourage you, a friend that invites you over, and makes you feel seen and heard? And all of this encouragement that this friend is lavishing on you motivates you to encourage and lavish love on others too? Friends like these not only care for you and your heart, but they also spur you on to do good for others, and the chain reaction continues to echo throughout the community that you are involved with, because being together and encouraging one another is contagious. I have been blessed by such friendships, and they are the most wonderful kinds of relationships. One of the biggest encouragements in my life right now actually brought up the idea of me writing this very devotional. I told her that I didn't think that I had much to offer; surely more educated, wiser, and spiritually healthier ladies were waiting in line to write devotionals. But, no, this friend brought it up time after time until I accepted the challenge and I never could have guessed how much of a blessing writing this devotional would be. The timing of this work and what I have been learning is how God has been caring for me, through his words in the Bible and the lessons he has asked me to share. I have never dug into the Word more deeply or for such long periods of time before preparing for this project.

I don't know that my friend realizes what a tremendous impact she has had in my life by asking me to join her in creating this devotional, but I am a different person now than when I first started this project. I am a stronger prayer warrior, a deeper lover of God's creation, a more patient person, and an ever-growing and maturing child of God. My friend helped me realize this by speaking the truth that she saw in me that I couldn't see for myself. She invited me into something bigger than both of us to further the kingdom. I cannot wait to see what God's work will do for those who love him.

ABBA,

Make me a selfless, strong encourager for my sisters and brothers around me. Thank you for those in my life who spur me on toward love and good deeds. Thank you for those in my life who have not given up on me and who pray for me. I am so grateful for their presence in my life. Allow me to help others serve you well, too.

AMEN.

Weekly Reflection

He WILL USe IT ALL

2 CORINTHIANS 9:8

And God is able to bless you abundantly, so that in all things at all times, having all that you need, you will abound in every good work.

2 Corinthians 9:8

Right after I graduated from college, I went on a missions trip to serve at an orphanage in Mexico. The college youth group that I was in had heard many wonderful stories about this orphanage because the pastors of our church were friends with the husband and wife who ran the orphanage and were working closely with them. The husband and wife weren't people of significant means but they loved Jesus, prayed all the time, and felt that God was asking them to help the children in their city who were in need. They obeyed his call without knowing exactly how they were going to do it. They had great faith in the Lord. God gave them the homes for the children and people who volunteered to care for the children each day. One particular day, God showed that he was truly going to cover every need.

The orphanage had no money for food and the husband and wife had been praying about their need for many days. On that particular morning, as they prayed with all of the children before a breakfast table with no breakfast, they heard a rumbling outside. A milk truck had broken down right in front of their home and had no way of getting fixed in time to deliver the milk before it spoiled, so the driver offered all of the milk to the orphanage. Next, a bread truck drove by, and little did those in the orphanage know, the truck had been driving around lost for quite some time. Eventually, the bread truck driver pulled over in front of the orphanage and offered the husband and wife the bread he had in his truck because it was past his delivery time. God had divinely sent the food that the orphanage needed that day right to its doorstep. He covered all of the orphanage's needs, and continued to provide just like this throughout the years for the husband and wife, and the children of the orphanage.

LORD,

Thank you for revealing yourself to me here on Earth, and helping me see you in tangible ways. Help me, Father, to trust you, and forgive me for worrying about things in my life instead of trusting you to provide. Strengthen me to look beyond myself and to be about your kingdom, so that I may serve where you direct me and give out of the abundance that you have given to me.

AMEN.

He Delights in Us

PSALM 18:19

He brought me out into a spacious place; he rescued me because he delighted in me.

Psalm 18:19

One night, I had a dream unlike any other. I dreamt that I was walking into a crowded coffee shop, weaving my way in between stuffed tables and book bags to an empty seat at a small wooden table where Jesus was sitting. I couldn't see his face but I knew that it was him because of the warmth and love exuding from him. I could feel that he was eagerly waiting for me to arrive and to sit with him. When I sat down, I just started talking to him and he drank in every word that I was saying. At that moment, I was the most important person to him and he wanted to hear all that I was sharing with him. Somehow I knew that every other person in the coffee shop was equally loved. I wasn't the only special person, but one among many.

After we were done talking, we both got up and I don't remember parting from him but I woke up with a jolt in my bed with tears of complete joy and adulation. I gently woke up my husband and shared my dream because I had to tell him of the love that I felt. I wanted him to know it too and I didn't want to forget any details.

I believe that Jesus visited me in my dream. I still cry when I recount this dream; the feeling of belonging to Jesus and being actively loved by him is beyond my ability to explain. The way he listened to me is an example that I can follow—to make someone feel loved, seen, and special by delightfully listening to whatever they are sharing with me. Our culture emphasizes taking care of ourselves, lifting our own voice and thoughts, and having people focus on us. The upside-down kingdom of Jesus demonstrates that believers are to lift up others, listen to others' thoughts, and to pay attention to them when they are sharing. Can you imagine what kind of love revolution we would start if we listened to others like Jesus listens to us?

ABBA,

I love you and praise you for your Son, Jesus Christ. Thank you for his example of how to live a good and worthy life here on earth and for how he loves me. Lord, help me to love all of your creation, to grow more aware of those around me, and to give them my attention and love. I love you, God. Thank you for loving me more than I can comprehend.

AMEN.

YOUR MIGHTY GIFTS

1 PETER 4:10

Each of you should use whatever gift you have received to serve others, as faithful stewards of God's grace in its various forms.

1 Peter 4:10

Jesus tells a parable of a master and three of his servants that he entrusts with talents, or wages, in Matthew 25:14–30.

A wealthy man gives three of his servants money to manage while the man is away. Each servant was given a different amount according to their ability. The first two servants received five and two talents, respectively, put their money to work, and doubled their amounts. But the third servant, who was given one talent, hid his money and gained nothing. The wealthy man was unhappy with that servant's actions and took the one coin talent and gave it to the servant who had been given five. The lesson for us is that God entrusts us with blessings and expects us to use our gifts wisely because he will be back and he will hold us accountable for how we use our gifts in this life.

Just like the talents were given according to each of the servants' abilities, God created us with different skills and abilities, too. He will assess what we do not by comparing his children to each other but how well we lived for His glory.

I have spent some time looking at some of my brothers' and sisters' lives and been pouty at what they got to do, what they received, what God was doing in their lives, and all the lack that was in my life. God was doing much in my life, but my attention was on what others had, and for a long time, I was acting like the servant with the one talent. But as God has corrected and grown me, showing me that while I was busy looking at other people, the blessings that were right in front of me were going to waste. I was squandering good things from God, and realizing that allowed me to focus back on God and prayerfully seek what he was asking me to do with what he had given to me.

I pray that you know that God has uniquely blessed you with gifts to bless the people in your community and to advance God's kingdom.

FATHER,

Thank you for knowing all of your children and for giving us each exactly what we need. Thank you for your patience with us and for your forgiveness. Help me to be about your work, Lord, and to do your will and not my own. Help me to see the gifts that you have blessed me with and to be a good steward of them for the good of others and to your glory.

AMEN.

HUMILITY ALWAYS WINS

JAMES 1:12

Blessed is the man who remains steadfast under trial, for when he has stood the test he will receive the crown of life, which God has promised to those who love him.

James 1:12

Many women in the Old Testament displayed wisdom, humility, loyal faithfulness, and leadership, considering others before herself. One example is Abigail, Nabal's wife. The soon-to-be King David extended aid to Nabal when Nabal was in need, but when David was on the run from a jealous King Saul and asked for food, Nabal refused to help him. David was livid and started toward Nabal's home to retaliate for his refusal to help. Nabal's wife Abigail heard about what was happening and took it upon herself to bravely go out to meet David on his way to her home, with supplies and an apology. She humbly presented herself with all of the food David needed and took the responsibility for her husband's mistake. She then informed David that if he continued with his plan, he would be making a grave mistake and would regret it once he became the king. Abigail spoke a prophetic word from God to David. She risked her life to save her family, her servants, and herself, but she was also helping advise David by reminding him of the truth that God had not called him to this fight with Nabal. David knew that Abigail had protected him from doing the wrong thing; if he killed Nabal, he would have been no better than Saul who was chasing after him. David praised Abigail and sent her safely back to her home with her servants. After Abigail told Nabal all that had happened, the Bible says that "his heart failed him and he became like a stone. About ten days later, the LORD struck Nabal and he died" (1 Samuel 25:37b-38).

Abigail showed herself to be a true and loyal leader; she "remained steadfast under trial." By acting in the way of wise peacemaking, Abigail honored God and her family in everything she did. Abigail was indeed a great hero because she proved to be incredibly faithful in her words and actions. Her actions were Christlike and honoring to God, even in the face of serious danger and possible death.

LORD,

You bless me when you give me opportunities to lead. Help me to honor you with my integrity and loyalty. Thank you for the example of your servant Abigail. Strengthen me with your wisdom. Allow me to be a worker who rightly handles the word of truth and honors you.

AMEN.

Too Much Grace

LAMENTATIONS 3:22–23

Certainly the faithful love of the Lord hasn't ended; certainly God's compassion isn't through! They are renewed every morning. Great is your faithfulness.

Lamentations 3:22–23

John 8 records the story of a woman who was caught in the act of adultery. The Pharisees and scribes brought her before Jesus and told him of her sin. Jesus stooped down and drew something on the ground and then responded to these religious men by making a bold statement: "The one without sin among you should be the first to throw the first stone at her" (John 8:7, CSB). When the Pharisees and the scribes heard this, they slowly started to walk away from the crowd. When Jesus stood back up, he spoke to the woman, "Woman, where are they? Has no one condemned you?" (John 8:10) The woman told Jesus that they hadn't and Jesus said, "Neither do I condemn you. Go, and from now on do not sin anymore" (John 8:11, CSB).

Jesus was not only extending grace and an invitation to this woman for redemption and reconciliation, who was a pawn in the attempts of the high-ranking Jewish religious elite to ensnare Jesus, but he was also extending the same invitation to the Pharisees and scribes who were attempting to destroy Jesus and this woman. Jesus is generous; he loves and is for every single one of us on earth, no matter how despicable we can be. Jesus didn't scold the woman for her sin, he didn't lecture the Pharisees for their hypocrisy and hardened hearts, and he didn't ask for the man who was also a part of the sin. Jesus showed us how we are to join him in ushering in the kingdom of God, with a humble and attentive heart and careful consideration to the person right in front of us. Jesus gave his time to this woman who was about to be put to death and he saved her from a horrible end.

I am sure we can all think of times when we have fallen into sin, or when we have witnessed others sin and maybe we haven't responded with generosity, help, or concern for others. What a reminder in this story that Jesus shows us to walk in the forgiveness of God and to not get taken down by what we have done. We need to ask for forgiveness and be reconciled to God, and to not sit in shame.

THANK YOU,

Father, for your lovingkindness and for your forgiveness. Help me to walk in the freedom that Jesus gave to me through his sacrifice. Thank you for your promise to me that "even the mountains may shift and the hills may be shaken, but your faithful love won't shift from me, and your covenant of peace won't be shaken" (Isaiah 54:10, paraphrased from CEB).

AMEN.

ABOUT THE AUTHOR

Des Leiloglou lives with her husband, Erastos, and her three daughters, Olivia, Eleni, and AviLouyah in San Antonio, Texas. Des enjoys eating the pebble ice in a gas station Dr Pepper while admiring old houses in and around her city. She also likes to decorate her family's home, hanging her daughters' original pieces of art on every wall, and organizing family adventures. On an average day, you can find Des talking with others about Jesus, hugging her husband, watching things grow in her garden, and homeschooling her daughters.